Strange As It May Seem

Compiled by
Karen Falk
as told by
Jethro Shaw

BY Pat Moran

A documentary of
the lives of
Ernest Bonaventure Moran
and His Daughter,
Patricia Grace Shaw
With Jethro Shaw

Strange As It May Seem

Memoirs of Patricia Moran Shaw & Ernest Bonaventure Moran

As told by Jethro Shaw

Compiled and written by
Karen B. Falk

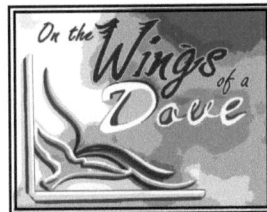

On the Wings of a Dove

Precious Fruit of the Earth

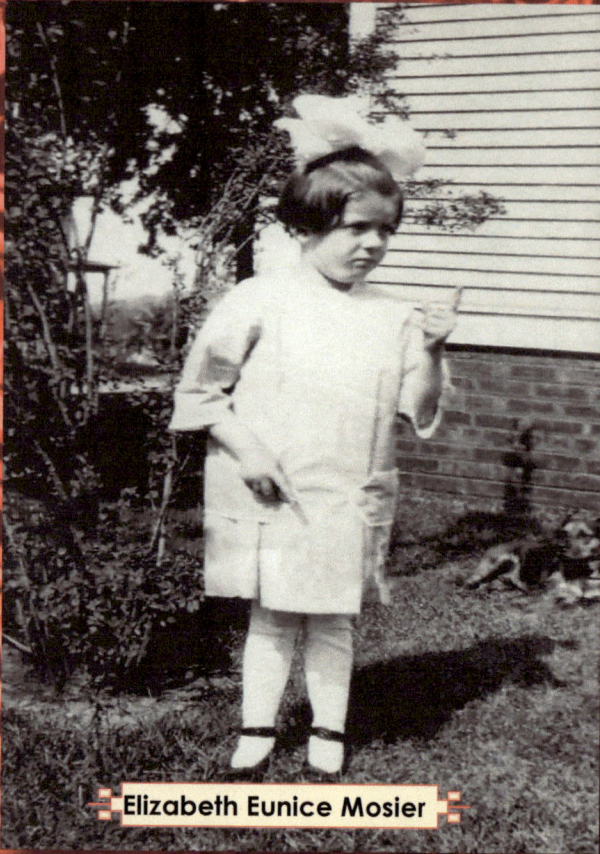

Elizabeth Eunice Mosier

Grace Brockway

Grace Brockway

Elizabeth Eunice Mosier

Elizabeth Eunice Mosier was born June 11, 1910 in Lewistown, Montana to a German man, William Mosier and to a Scotch- Irish woman, Elizabeth O'Grady.

It was believed that Elizabeth was born in a small town in Indiana.

Elizabeth (O'Grady) Mosier died when her daughter Betsy was three. Betsy's father left them and disappeared until his death was reported back to them years later. Aunt Grace Brockway stepped in to raised Betsy and her older brother. Grace was ill at times and it was costly to raise Betsy, who was often sick. Mr. Brockway, Betsy's uncle provided for them. When Betsy was five, he passed away.

Heart problems took their toll on Betsy, and by the time she was in 6th grade in school, she was unable to climb the school stairs. She had to drop out of school, and Grace used all that was left of Mr. Brockway's money to take care of Betsy.

CERTIFIED COPY OF RECORD OF BIRTH

STATE OF MICHIGAN,
County of Mason.
Ludington, Michigan

I, Jerome A. Jorissen, Clerk of the County of Mason and of the Circuit Court thereof, the same being a Court of Record having a seal, do hereby certify that the following information is from the record of Birth of Ernest Moran now remaining in my office, via:

CHILD

RECORD NO.	DATE OF BIRTH			SURNAME AND CHRISTIAN NAME (IF ONE BE GIVEN)	MALE OR FEMALE	WHITE, BLACK, MULATTO, ETC.
	MONTH	DATE	YEAR			
3-239	June	1	1903	Ernest Moran	M	W

STILL-BORN, ILLEGITIMATE, TWINS, ETC.	BIRTH PLACE	LOCAL FILE NO.
	Ludington, Michigan	3-239

PARENTS

FULL NAMES OF EACH	RESIDENCE	BIRTH PLACE OF EACH
William Moran	Ludington, Michigan	Canada
Elizabeth Moran	Ludington, Michigan	Michigan

Occupation of Father Brakeman Date of Record May 26, 1904

In Testimony Whereof, I have hereunto set my hand and affixed the seal of said Circuit Court, the 12th day of March A. D., 19 70 Jerome A. Jorissen Clerk.

JEROME A. JORISSEN
By _____ Deputy Clerk.

William Moran, was a Canadian brakeman from Michigan. The Moran name is derived from Ireland and French, William wed to a French woman- Elizabeth Fontaine of Ludington, Michigan.

William and Elizabeth had a total of seventeen children. Six of the babies died at, or near birth. Ernest Bonaventure Moran was next to the youngest out of eleven, and he was placed into an orphanage.

When Ernest was born, June 1, 1903, the old lighthouse on the south pier of Muskegon Lake was renovated from wood to metal, and for the first time the light was steadily lit for 511 hours. It used 43 tons of coal and three chords of wood. That special event was September 27, 1903.

When Ernest was ten, he started working to make his own living. He got out of the orphanage and needed a place to stay.

"Come live with me," one brother said, when they met on the street. Ernie's troubles of homelessness were over.

- Nations will come to your light, and kings the brightness of your rising. Isaiah 60:3

Ernie with 2 recruits when he was in the Army Air Corps

Ernie and a relative, Ethel, on his first enlistment

Ernie on border patrol.

Ernie and enlisted men in the Texas National Guard

Ernie with his plane

In 1916, when Ernest (or Ernie) was thirteen years old, he enlisted in the armed forces. As was common during the era of WW1, Young men wanted to grow up fast and be involved in defending their country.

General Mac Arthur was chief of staff and commander of the 42nd Division of the 87th Brigade (The Rainbow Division) Army Infantry during WW1 occupation at the time when Ernie signed into the army and began to serve in 1916.*

Ernie served the Texas National Guard defending the Mexican border by Calvary during World War I.

The government sent Ernie home when they found out the truth about his age.

The Paris Peace Conference finalized and approved. They presented a treaty to Germany in May 1919. On June 11, 1919, Ernie re-enlisted into the military. This time, he was 16 years old when he enlisted in the Army Air Corps. (Which eventually became the United States Air Force), right before Germany was under the threat of invasion from the Allied countries. It was signed at the Palace of Versaille near Paris, on June 28, 1919.*

At the same time, Douglas Mac Arthur was appointed to be Brigadier General of the National Army.*

Ernie served the army for three more years. He was a private of Headquarters Detachment of the 1st Pursuit Group, Air Service, in Selfridge Field, Michigan, until his honorable discharge on August 17, 1922. He had become a member of the 94th Aero Squadron, Eddie Rickenbacker's Squadron First Pursuit Squad, and was commended from Service Force Seven Fleet- "Admiral Kinkaid's Own."

By May 1924, Ernie had started working as a recruiter for the Texas National Guard, that consisted of the 36th Division, and the 42nd (Rainbow) Division, serving in the Air Force when it was still part of the Army Signal Corps.

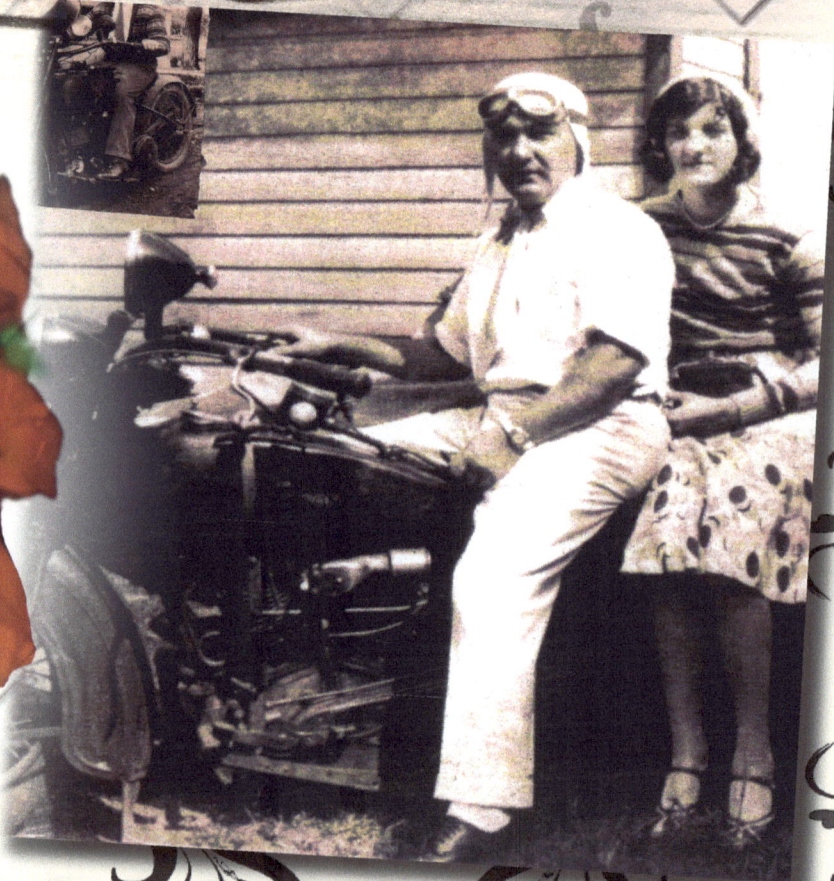

On September 25, 1926, Ernie Moran and Betsy Fontaine got married by a justice of the peace, Justice, V. Fulton. They were two kids who loved to ride the motorcycle. Betsy was a clerical worker. Ernie was a sign painter from Houston, Texas. She must have been sweet sixteen, although the marriage certificate says she was eighteen, the date on the marriage license and the date of her birth tell a different story. Ernie was twenty-three years old when they got married in his brother, Frank's home. Betsy met her groom in a green satin dress with a bouquet of roses. Forty people came to the wedding reception and supper. Even though they had both been orphans, they started a new life together.

Betsy had a brother, and a sister. Her brother's name was Verdin, and he had moved to Kalamazoo, Michigan, where her aunt-Mrs. Harry Cooper, lived also. Betsy had a sister also (name unknown), who married Walter Geist of 485 Octavus St., also of Muskegon, Michigan.

Betsy was baptized and confirmed in the First English Evangelical Lutheran Church of Muskegon, at a Pentecostal Service. She was well thought of by the parishioners.

These pictures appear to be Elizabeth Fontaine Moran or "Betsy" in different scenes of her life.

Muskegon, with a county population of 37,000 at the turn of the century when Ernest Moran was born, was the "Riviera of the Midwest," and "the lumber capital of the world." Chicago had been rebuilt from Muskegon lumber after the great fire.. There were 47 lumber saw mills established on Muskegon Lake (the port to Lake Michigan) by the mid 1880's and 16 along White Lake, nearby to the north, but in 1929, the last sawmill closed and Muskegon was becoming industrial based.

Mercy Hospital opened downtown in the former L.G. Mason mansion on Jefferson St. in 1903, and that is where Patricia Grace Moran was born. On March 7, 1935 at Mercy Hospital in Muskegon, Michigan, she came, as beautiful and gracious as one of the flowers that Betsy loved so well.

Under the circumstances of her birth- to a mother who battled sickness her whole life, and a father who forged against all that life had to offer before he had reached adulthood, Pat's birth was an unusual event. But it did happen, she graced the world with her presence, - a tiny pearl of the vast harbor, and more precious than the sand of the shore.

Patricia was their only child, and Betsy loved children so, she must have loved Patricia twice as strongly. Pat was the apple of her father's eye.

Pictured on the left are Patricia Moran as a baby with both of her parents.

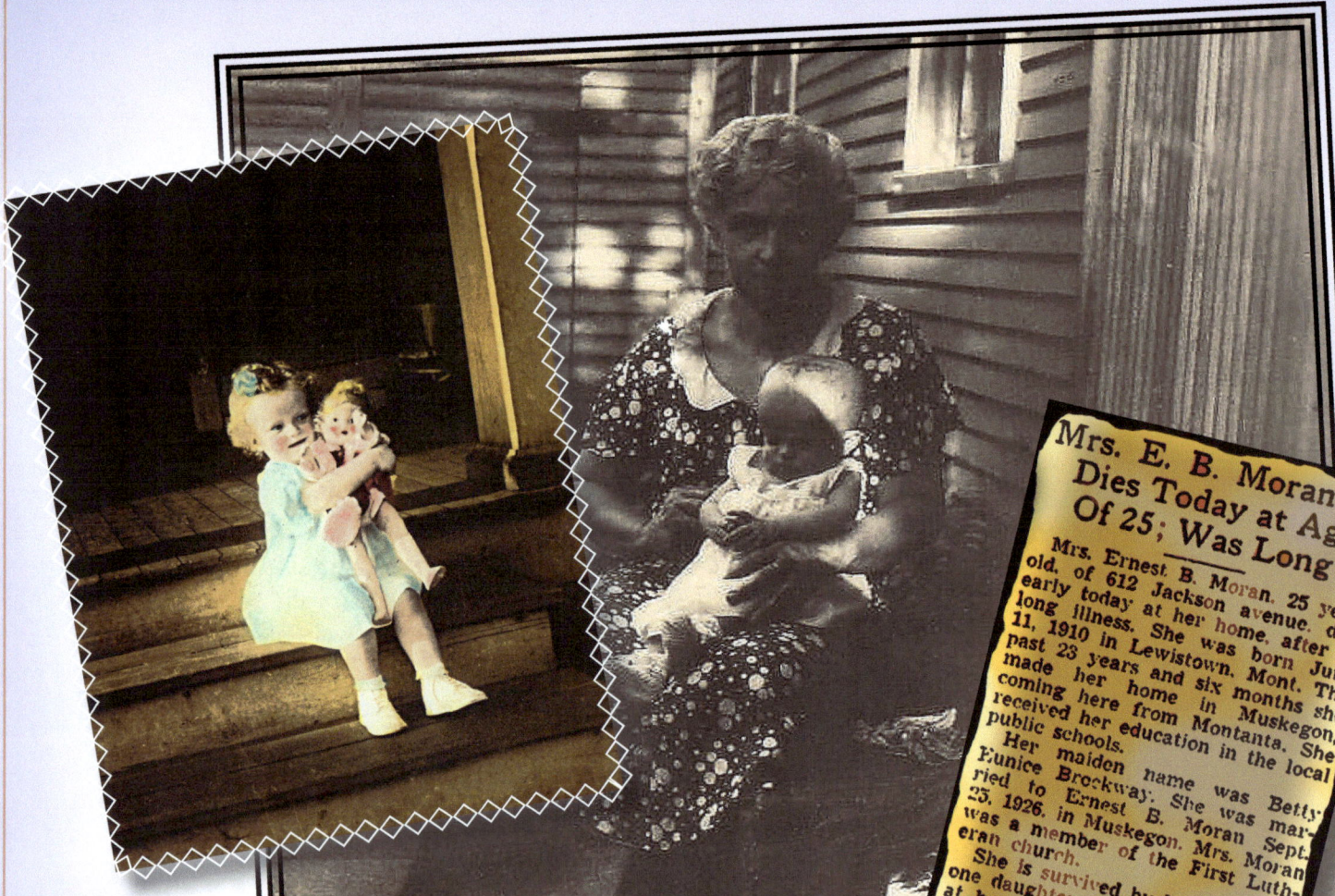

Grace Brockway & baby Pat

On November 25, 1935, Betsy's heart failed after life-long illness and she passed away. 612 Jackson Avenue, Muskegon, Michigan, was not the same.

The following poem was written by her friend, Mrs. Edna L. Inman:

OUR FRIEND

Our dear friend, how we miss her
Since she has passed beyond.
We know she is happy there,
But still our heart does mourn.

Some day we hope to meet her,
In that home so very fair,
And we pray her darling baby
Will also meet her there.

Death is a sad example
Of how we leave this earth.
Our days here are numbered
From the moment of our birth.

Betsy's great aunt Grace, who raised her, moved in to help care for Patricia. Patricia loved her Great Aunt Grace, dearly.

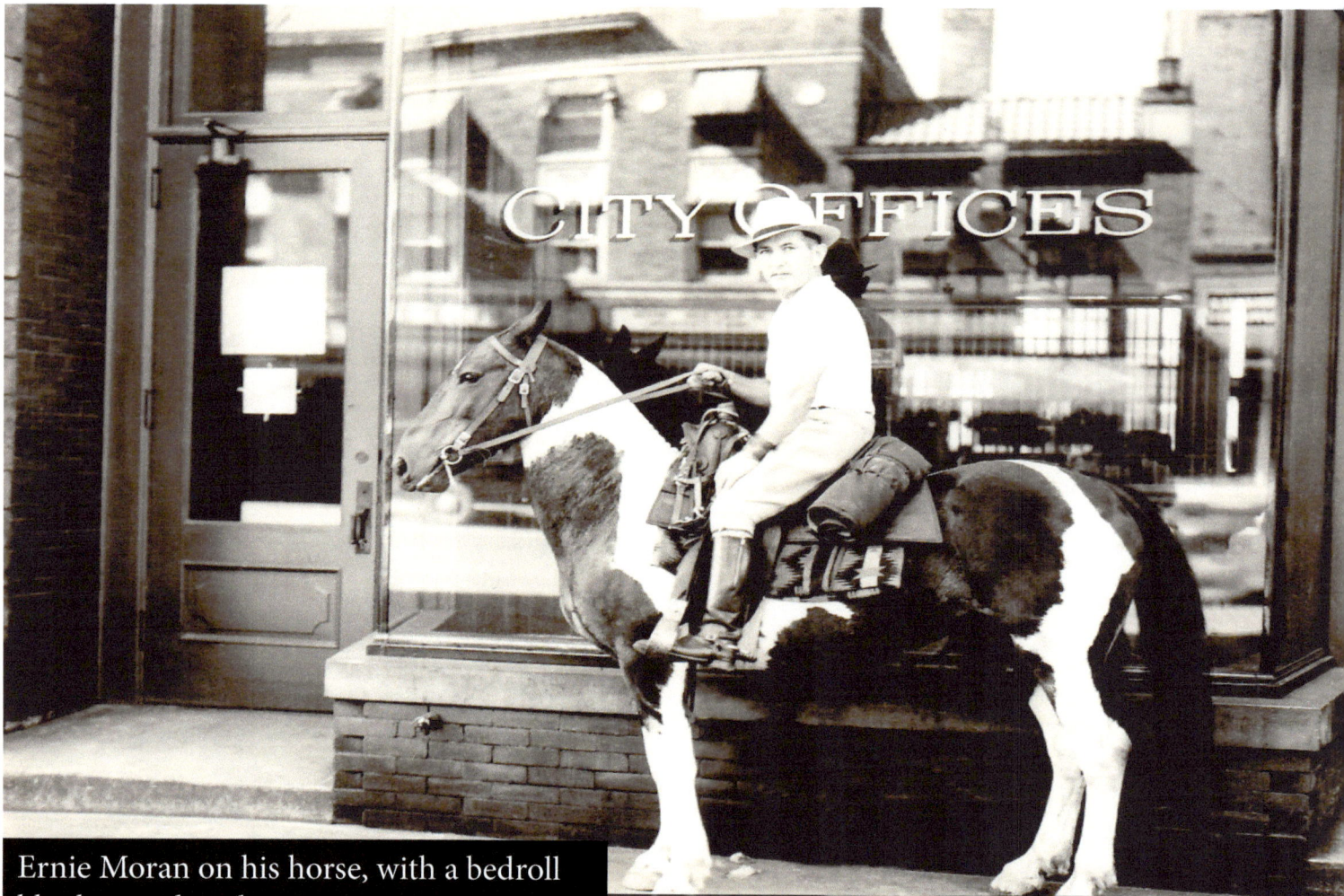

Ernie Moran on his horse, with a bedroll blanket, and pack.

In the fall of one year while Pat was a small child, Ernest bought a 4 year old horse and ventured to ride across the United States. The West was calling, and he could not refuse.

He'd been a sign writer at Henry Day since spring, painting signs. Maybe his pinto was named "Paint" for a that very reason.

He was an experienced traveler by motorcycle and car, and he felt the trip would be successful if he cared for his little horse. Ernie packed a blanket and a horse first aid kit, as well as a grooming kit. The plans were drawn up- grand plans to ride across the country in 5 years. With 25 miles a day and a few days' rations, he could travel light.

HORSE AND RIDER OFF ON LONG TRIP AROUND COUNTRY

With many thousands of miles and five years of travel before them, Ernest B. Moran and his horse, "Paint," left at 10 o'clock Sunday morning for a horseback trip around the United States which, Mr. Moran hopes, will bring him back to Traverse City in 1938.

Carrying only a light saddle pack, horse and rider departed from the city hall while a good sized crowd cheered them.

Mr. Moran,, who has previously made motorcycle and automobile trips about the country, questions if his little western horse can complete the trip. He will favor him all the way, however, in an effort to make him last out the five years.

Sunday night Mr. Moran planned to spend at Kingsley and from there he will hit US-131 and continue south to Grand Rapids and thence to Chicago. From there he has no plans other than to hit northwest.

Ernie left 3 year old Patsy with friends and started out from City Hall on East Front St. in Traverse City, Michigan. It was Sunday morning at 10:00 A.M. when he said his good-byes to the standing crowd.

"I'll see you in five years," he said as he waved and rode off toward Grand Rapids, Michigan.

His plans were to travel to Kingsley, then via US-131 to Grand Rapids and Chicago, then through the Northwest.

After reaching Cedar Springs, Ernie spent the day there, and led the Homecoming Parade. It was then on to Reed City.

He tethered Paint to a pole and went off to rest, only to hear hoof beats on pavement soon after. Checking to see, he discovered his equine protégé had escaped. Ernie chased Paint for half an hour until was caught.

Ernie had high hopes, to travel onward to Chicago, along the Mississippi Valley to Texas, then on to California. He didn't quite make the whole trip. Who knows where he ended up. The trip itself clearly demonstrates the determination and strong willed character of young Ernest Moran.

Ernie is pictured with young Pat, who must have been about two years old here.

Ernest Moran photo of Hawaii

SS MONTERY [Photograph found in MATSON PASSENGER
ERA , Matson, Hawaii]. (n.d.). Retrieved from https://www.mat-
son.com/bos/img/history/0301b_450x223.jpg
https://www.matson.com/bos/history_sec0301.shtml

Ernest ordered a ticket to board the S.S. Matsonia, from the Mart Travel Bureau, got in his car and drove with three year old Patsy to San Francisco, California. He courageously left everything that he knew to travel to a new land and future with little possessions, with his little daughter, and with the American Dream.

Beginning March 13, 1939 at 5:00 P.M. they crossed the ocean to Honolulu, Hawaii- a two week trip. In Hawaii, he hoped to raise his daughter without the disapproval and the cultural bias of that time. It was unacceptable for a single man to raise a daughter, during the era between the great wars.

On a side note, the SS. Matsonia passenger ship soon after their trip, was converted to a war vessel and was used to participate in World War 2. The USS Matson.

"BEGINNING A NARRATIVE POEM OF HAWAII

(Author unknown)
Attributed to E.B Moran

Impatient feet that paced the deck are stilled
And eager eyes that gaze at Diamond Head are filled.
The straining heart would fain the ship empower,
With flight to see old Punchbowl and Aloha Tower;
For dreams long cherished so dear to heart come true-
With first far-glimpse of this enchanting view;
And faintly borne on Trade wind soft and low,
The "Song of the Islands" comes with ebb and flow
Of Hawaii-- The Land of the Open Door!
And here the breeze is perfume laden, too;
The garden of the world sends out its spell to woo-
All foreigners –soon willing slaves they'll be
To this volcanic isle that rests upon the sea.

At dam of Lei Day we come to port,
In very shadow of great Ruger Fort!
We learn what welcome means from those who meet
The ships bestowing ginger wreathes so white and sweet
Saw poinciana and illema lei royal
Against those dark hued throats a perfect foil
But loved the best, the feathered lei blue
Who rare and brilliant loveliness few knew.

I found an Oriental garden there,
Where once the lava beds made all things bare
Hawaiian waters with their limpid blue
Reflect the blossoms' colors of rainbow hue
Where singing birds of rippling water make
A song that fills your heart with Love's own ache.
For love of beauty unappeased in man
Approach perfection in this jeweled fan.
The sweetness of the morning still asleep
In the still light of stars that nightly keep
Unwavering watch o'er this rare, lovely place
Where white hibiscus bloom, and shadows trace.
A twisted trellis of bougainvillea vine--
The morning mist subdues its splendor fine.
To harmony with neighboring blues and pinks
Of seeming shyer flowers which nods and winks
At the Spirit of the Garden, as he sips
From dew-filled cups"

Ace High
SIGNS

WINDOW and TRUCK LETTERING — BANNERS — SHO-CARDS

PICTORIAL — WINDOW DISPLAY — DESIGNING — INSIGNIAS

TER

GENERAL
Building
Paintin
Mason
A LIBRA

ASK FOR
LITERAT

Calling ALL MERCHANTS "ATTENTION" Introducing..... Honolulu's latest "Advertiser" 'Covers the Island' MADE & SERVICED by Ace High Signs

TONG · CHOCK
SIGNS
TELEPHONE · 5285
Cottage No. 5 · KAUMAKAPILI LANE

Acme
& Designs 2-7578

PERMIT CARD
Painters, Paperhangers & Decorators
Local No. 475 of Muskegon
Name Ernest Moran
Work From Date April 21
To Date May 3
Signed Charles Gary

Holiday
Greetings and
"Aloha"
From Utility Squadron One

MORAN & Signs

E&B. MORAN

Ernest and Patsy outside of the sign shop

Ernest, who was an artist, a sign maker and graphic designer by trade, started his own sign business on March 29, 1939. It was Ace High Signs. Ernie's business had two locations, one at 1415 Kinan St. Box 42 and the other at 1378 S. King and Keeaumoku Streets, in Honolulu, Hawaii.

Ernie borrowed $150.00 from the Liberty Bank of Honolulu to make the trip and get his business started. He paid it back fully and on time, for $15.00 per month with no interest.

接寫招牌 TONG · CHOCK 唐卓

SIGNS

TELEPHONE · 5285

Cottage No. 5 · KAUMAKAPILI LANE
On Beretania Street Bet., Nuuanu and Smith

Acme Designs

Phone 2·7578

INDUSTRIAL · COMMERCIAL
· PICTORIAL
· AIR BRUSH
· SIGNS

E B MORAN
468 W HACKLEY

LP A HARRINGTON
MUSKEGON HEIGHTS

PERMIT CARD

Painters, Paperhangers & Decorators

Local No. 475 of Muskegon

Name _Ernest Moran_

Work From—Date _April 21_

To—Date _May 3 – 1939_

Signed _Charles Cary_

Business Agent

CITY AND COUNTY OF HONOLULU
DEPARTMENT OF BUILDINGS

A. W. HEEN
Superintendent of Buildings

HONOLULU, HAWAII

June 15, 1939

Ace-High Signs
1378 S. King Street
Honolulu, T. H.

Gentlemen:

Representatives of the Outdoor Circle appeared before the Public Works Committee of the Board of Supervisors on June 9, 1939, and urged that an ordinance be passed to restrict the size of store signs. After hearing their proposal, the Committee invited them to confer with me in working out a possible amendment to the Building Code embracing their suggestion.

Pursuant to the Committee's action, I have called a meeting of interested groups for 3:00 p. m. Monday, June 19, in the City Hall assembly room for a preliminary discussion of the Outdoor Circle's proposal.

Your company, which would be affected by any plan to limit the size of signs, is cordially invited to send a representative to the meeting. I believe that suggestions and opinions expressed at this meeting would be helpful to all parties concerned.

Very truly yours,

A. W. Heen
Superintendent of Buildings

AWH:tk

BUSINESS AND PROFESSIONAL MEN'S COOPERATIVE
CLUB OF HONOLULU

April 7, 1939.

Dear Members:

The next scheduled meeting of the Business and Professional Men's Cooperative Club of Honolulu will be held in the club rooms of the Army-Navy Y.M.C.A., on the evening of Tuesday, April 11, 1939, at 8:00 p.m.

There is enclosed herewith a copy of the Constitution for your perusal. Amendments will be discussed at the next meeting.

The President has directed me to advise you of the following committee appointments named by him:

MEMBERSHIP	INVESTIGATING	CLASSIFICATION
Mr. E. B. Moran	Mr. T. F. Allen	Mr. T. W. Gibson
Mr. W. H. Lichter	Mr. G. Seitz	Mr. E.B. Moran
Mr. T. W. Gibson	Mr. C. L. Carrell	Mr.L.Yelman.

For the information of the members there is listed below the classification, business and addresses of the present members:

Mr. W. J. Feeley, Churchill's Ltd., Furniture Mart, Beretania and Alakea St., Tel #6280.
Mr. J. Edwin Whitlow, Attorney at law, and President Honolulu Business College, 1176 Fort St., Tel. #3940.
Mr. E. B. Moran, Sign Painter, displays, etc. Ace-High Signs, 1378 S. King St.,Tel #5435.
Mr. C. L. Carrell, electrician and apartments, 2008 Kinau St., Tel. #77380.
Mr. G. H. Malone, accountant, c/o Mr. W. Feeley.
Mr. T. F. Allen, painter, decorator, etc., Honolulu Piano Shop, 1800 S. King St.,
Mr. G. Seitz, commercial photographer, c/o Mr. L. Yelman
Mr. T. W. Gibson, new & used cars, c/o Murphy Motors.
Dr. W. H. Lichter, physician & surgeon,Tel #7996.
Mr.R. Feary, account and tax expert, 401 Bishop Bank Bldg., Tel #8746.
Mr. L. Yelman, 1216 S. Sierra Drive, Real estate broker. Tel #77092.

SECRETARY.

He also worked for the Governor of Hawaii, guarding the island by pursing criminals that fled and hid in the uncharted mountains of Hawaii, a land that was still an unfamiliar territory to most of the people in the United States.

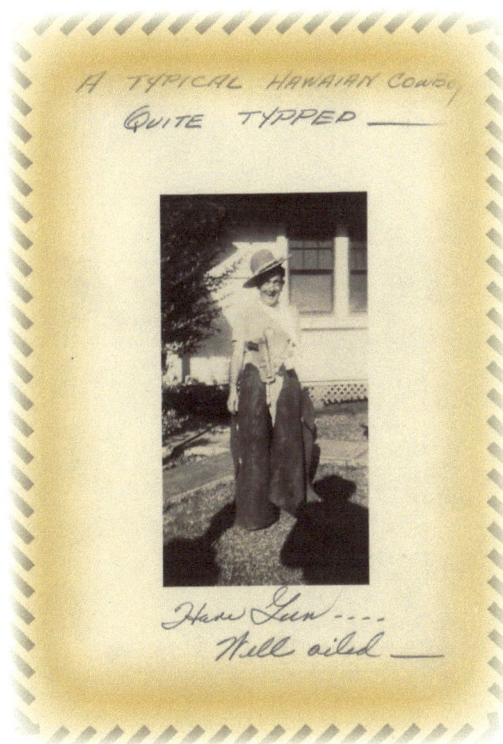

A TYPICAL HAWAIAN COWBOY
QUITE TYPPED ___

Have Gun....
Well oiled ___

The photographs featured here and on the next two pages depict Ernie in various scenes. Most of them include the horses that he rode.

Ernest Moran on the rink and ready to play hockey with his team, the Royal Rollers

1939

CHRISTMAS

AND SINCERE GOOD WISHES FOR THE COMING YEAR

Mr. & Mrs. Frank Willard.

A Christmas card from Mr. & Mrs. Frank Willard

GREETINGS

PLAY TONIGHT: The Civic Royal Rollers, pictured above, will meet the Wahiawa Hawks in a roller hockey game at the Civic auditorium tonight. From left to right, those in the picture are: Front row—F. Fair, utilities; J. Ehling, utilities; E. Moran, goalie (acting manager); E. Donnelly, utilities; R. Chillingworth, center. Rear row—T. Thompson, left wing; D. Bernard, right forward; M. Reed, right wing (acting captain); L. Spiering, utilities; C. Lund, left forward (acting coach). Not in picture—Benny Bennett, utilities.

Ernest became Scoutmaster of Boy Scout Troop 134 while in Pearl City, Oahu. A perfect fit- for the Boy Scouts Organization taught young men commitment and service to their country.

Ernie's apparent love for the game of hockey showed, in that he became the acting manager and goalie of the Hawaiian roller hockey team, the Civic Royal Rollers Club of 1939. Prior to the trip to Hawaii, he was in the Ambassadors Skate Club in April of 1929, As well as the Coliseum Roller Skating Rink of Traverse City.

Ernie, not only a graphic designer and sign painter, but also a fine artist and woodworker submitted at least one of his paintings to art exhibition. One of his paintings, an oil painting entitled "Senorita," hung in the center gallery of the 12th Annual Exhibition of Work by Artists of Muskegon and Vicinity, at the Hackley Art Gallery in February 1938. The Hackley Art Gallery, dedicated to Muskegon by multi-millionaire lumber lord Charles H. Hackley, is now called the Muskegon Museum of Art.

Mr. & Mrs. Taber

Ana D. Taber & Pat

Mr. Taber & Pat

Pat in various scenes

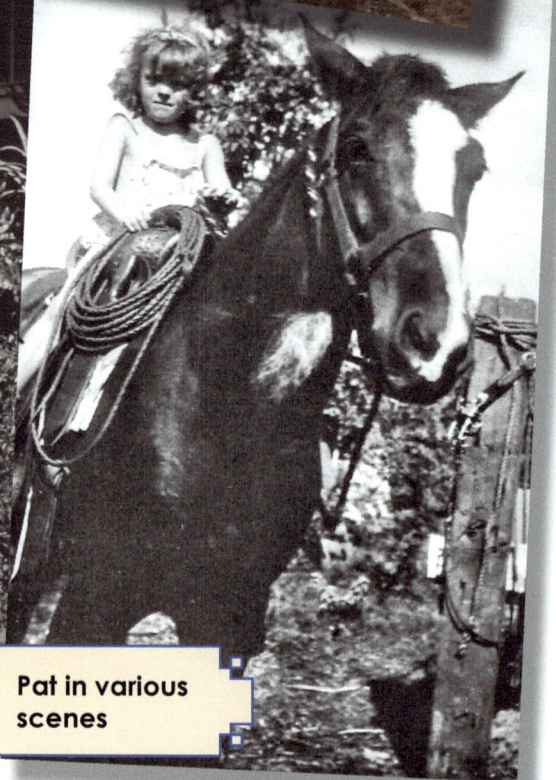

A fair child with curls of golden hair, living in a place where the people native to the land have dark hair and dark eyes, Pat was favored by the natives of the land. They gave her candy and gifts.

Pat had already experienced more in her young life than many in their adulthood- having lost her mother, leaving her Aunt Grace, staying with various caregivers while her father was away, then traveling to a distant land aboard a steamship, - she was the child of a military man, and perhaps that in itself as well as all these circumstances helped to make her strong. She soon had more fearful experiences in her young life.

In one of her school writings, Pat explained that her dad came home from work one day, in order to check on her. He entered his home just in time to rescue her from certain death. The woman who took care of her was trying to drown Pat in the bathtub.

After that, (Jethro, her husband shared) that Pat experienced trauma whenever anything covered her face. She screamed in fear when a dress became tight around her neck as it was pulled over her head, and the collar had to be cut with shears.

From then on, Pat was entrusted with a new couple, Mr. and Mrs. Anna D. Taber, of Honolulu, who were of Russian descent. They cared for Pat while Ernie was at work. As a small child, Mrs. Taber nick-named her "Patsy." Pat called her "Mama Taber." They lived at 1315 Lunalilo St., Honolulu, T. H., and had a son named Gene Taber.

Anna Taber was rich in faith toward God, and full of love for Pat, as is found in her later writings to Viola Davis. She was a very kind soul. The Tabers continued to help Ernie and be part of his life while he traveled to Honolulu during military endeavors in later years. Anna wrote about Ernie's visit to Hawaii in her letter to Viola Davis in 1944 after an unfortunate circumstance.

Pictured on the opposite page are Mr. and Mrs. Taber with Patsy in Hawaii.

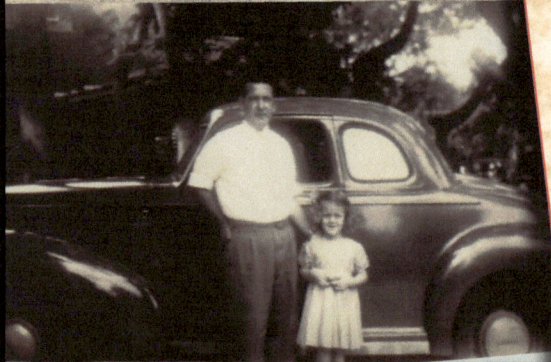

Ernie took to being mom and dad for Pat. He managed their home and did the laundry, cooking and cleaning. When he wasn't at work. He brushed and curled Pat's beautiful blonde hair into ringlets and made sure she was well dressed and cared for.

Pat displayed an independent streak while very young, "… when I was just learning to walk around, I would dig into a loaf of bread with my fist and soon it would look like the mice had been at work," she stated in her high school biography.

She learned to use the scissors, then attempted to cut her own hair, "Like most children do..." she wrote.

Once, when her father had been painting buildings, Pat climbed his tallest ladder to the top. Frightened by the sight of her on top of the ladder he used to paint "High Signs" on buildings, Ernie cautiously scaled the ladder to get her down before she fell to a certain death.

The pictures included here show Patsy, growing up in Hawaiian with her dad.

Top left : Pat in a grass skirt,
Top right: natives in grass
skirts
Middle left: Pat at Wakiki
Beach.
Middle right: Pat and new
puppy
Bottom left and center:
Pat practicing hockey
on roller skates.

It has been said, "When in Rome, do as the Romans." Pat while growing up in Hawaii, learned the culture of the Hawaiian people. She learned to speak their language, and Japanese, as well as English.

Pat must have greatly overcome her fears- of her early experience with near drowning, in order to enjoy sunbathing on Waikiki Beach. A nice afternoon in the sun would turn into danger when a sudden wave swept Pat out into the ocean rife with many sharks and other man eating fish. As small as she was it is a wonder she didn't drown, let alone get devoured by a carnivorous fish! No wonder the natives were such skillfully seasoned and avid swimmers!

It seems, Pat always had a pet dog. At one time, Pat said in her writing, she discovered some of the natives really liked her dog. They enjoyed it for a meal. Needless to say, it was a good reason for Pat's dad to buy her a new puppy.

In Hawaii, Pat, like her father was an avid skater, as is shown in the pictures on the opposite page. She was very good and professional, having learned to skate at a very young age. Ernie loved to play hockey and taught Pat how to play.

Pat began attending school in Hawaii. The school was about a block from their home. She attended there until one day, a major catastrophe occurred.

Ernie Moran was stationed at the U.S. Naval Air Station on Ford Island, according to newspaper articles.

According to her cousin and friend, for years it was rumored that Pat was on the military boat with her dad on that fateful day in December.

Those details are left to imagination, unless something- some document, exists, or if someone who was there should remember all the details.

According to Patricia's account from her school writings, she was with Mr. and Mrs. Taber, who were looking after her.

*In May 1941, the Pacific Fleet based at Pearl Harbor and commanded by Admiral Husband E. Kimmel consisted of 9 battleships, 3 aircraft carriers, 12 heavy and 8 light cruisers, 50 destroyers, 33 submarines, and 100 patrol bombers. The strength of the fleet was substantially the same on Dec. 7, 1941.. (*THE FALL OF THE PHILIPPINES)

Pat wrote that she was riding her tricycle when her Russian caregivers yelled from the house. Ignoring the beckon to come inside, she continued her ride, until Pat and the pilot of the foreign plane saw eye to eye. She had no fear, but she went inside.

The bombs were dropped a block from their home. Pat stated that she was unafraid on December 7, 1941, the day that the Pearl Harbor was attacked by Japanese bomb pilots.

She was unable to attend school after that. The school no longer existed.

Ernest became a member of the Hawaiian Territorial Guard -the state of Hawaii's defense force to protect the island during WW11. He was answerable only to the governor of Hawaii and could not be deployed to serve elsewhere. He rode his horse across Hawaii to keep watch over the island to protect and preserve the freedom of others. His weapon of defense would have been the M-1903 Springfield rifle. He was to guard the Island from potential ground attack from Japanese soldiers.

Ernie, was compelled to active duty as a special investigator for the Coast Guard on the West Coast.

On the left, upper- Pat is on her tricycle, probably an early picture of her first ride.
The upper middle: she is standing on the busy sidewalk in front of "The Cherry," The third shows Pat in a gas mask from the air raid at Pearl Harbor.
Again, in the lower middle picture, Pat is on her beloved trike, which she continued to fearlessly ride.
On the bottom left appears a younger Ernie Moran, in front of his car in a Naval uniform and coat.
On the bottom right, Pat is in front of the Island airways plane that may have taken her to California after Pearl Harbor was bombed.

Pat, like her father, enjoyed horses.

Before his full active duty in the Navy, Ernie advertised the need for a caregiver for his child in the San Francisco paper.

Jerome and Viola Davis of 1017 East Alisal St., Salinas, California answered the ad, and Ernie went active.

Jerome, Viola, Pat and Judy (a Collie dog) moved to Portales, New Mexico. The family was living in a 6 room house. In April 1944, Viola wrote to Ernie (through v-mail) that Patty had started school there, and they were and awaiting her papers from Washington. Jerome, or "Jerry" bought a 40 acre farm that was 18 miles from Clovis, and 95 miles from Roswell, New Mexico. He paid $65.00 per acre. With a down payment of $500.00 and a payment of $300.00 per year. Pat was treated as a member of the family. Ernie was included and he treated them well, sending money for Pat and helping out the Davis's as they had need in their endeavors. Jerry planted crops of corn and peanuts.

"-Because peanuts are a good money crop," Mrs. Davis wrote in her letter to Ernie Moran. They also raised cows and chickens.

The family commuted to the farm from town until their cement basement home was finished enough for them to live. They worked together to build a basement, moved in and planned to eventually build upper quarters. The upper part of their home was never completed. The family was contented in their circumstance and were hard working, congenial, faith loving, and happy.

They lived in their basement home for the duration of the war, while Ernie was active in the Navy.

Ernie became employed by the Salinas Army Air Base, before he enlisted in the See Bees, then served General MacArthur, as chief cartographer, preparing for war in the Philippines Islands.

Jerome and Viola Davis

1944 was quite a year. Pat was nine. She liked school and walked every school day. She liked spelling and felt she was not as talented with math.

In May, Pat had gotten a pet chicken. She found she liked the taste of roasted peanuts, which sold for 5 cents a bag.

In June, Pat writes to her dad about her love of sweet corn, and her two pet kittens. Pat writes of helping the Davis's water the corn crop and work clods out of the dirt so the irrigation pump water could flow, getting herself stuck in mud.

In July, Pat received a pretty card from her Daddy and a doll. She was excited to visit to Electra, Texas to see Mrs. Davis' ill mother and sister, and visit their two girls.

Pat learned to clean house and cook, with Mrs. Davis at her side. Mrs. Davis, or Auntie as she was called by Pat, had a reputation for being a good cook.

At one time during the year, (Pat told her teacher in her high school writing assignment) she tried to light the stove and threw the lighted match in the trash, which caught on fire. The fire licked up and burned the kitchen curtains.

Pat Moran & Judy

Pat in her new suit, with her dad.

Pat is pictured here with Ernie during and after her illness. The paper in the bottom right corner is a copy of the leave of absence that Ernie applied for.

CEMENT DEPOT

LEAVE OF ABSENCE

Authority for ~~urgent~~ emergency leave of absence from this station is granted to:

M O R A N,   Ernest Bonaventure   378 49 77   CCM(T)
Last Name   First   Middle   Service No.   Rate

From _____ 7 September 1944 1100 _____ To _____ 7 October 1944 1100
Day   Month   Hour   Day   Month   Hour

Address while on leave—Care of_____ Clovis Army Air Base Hospital _____
Street Address

Albuquerque, _____ New Mexico _____
City   State   Telephone No.

Leave authorized by_____ COMMANDER W.H. RANDER CEC USN.
Type name and rank of officer granting leave

Leave authority issued by_____ R.J. _____ Lt. (jg) D-V(S) USNR.
Signature of Personnel Officer or O. O. D.

Bag and personal gear checked_____
Signature of M. A. A.

Logged out by O. O. D._____
Time   Date   Signature and rank

Logged in by O. O. D._____
Time   Date   Signature and rank

NOTICE—Prepare in triplicate; all papers to be returned to leave yeoman, Personnel Department, when leave
is completed.

(See reverse side for regulations)

Pat tried to extinguish the fire with a dipper of water. "Auntie" (Pat's endearing term for Mrs. Davis) came just in time to prevent their kitchen from burning.

In Mrs. Davis airmail letter to Ernie she mentions, "I never let her fool with fire, or hot water while I am away. But she often helps cook and other things when I am home."

During the month of May, in 1944, Pat began to feel ill at school- a temporary condition, it seemed. She soon got better. Then suddenly, things took a turn for the worse. Usually a good student in school, her grades started to slip. Pat had begun to lose eyesight in one eye, and then more slowly, the other. She failed in school. By the time the fall season came with its bounty, Pat was blind.

Doctors at the Clovis Air Base Hospital determined the treatment for Pat would required 63 shots of penicillin.

Her dad was right there by her side, when the nurses came with the needles. The shots made her feel fear, and tearful. Her dad played checkers with her, and ate meals with her. Pat was cheered by the attention.

Although she felt like crying. She laughed when her dad joked about feeding peanuts to Judy, the dog. Pat looked forward to a new puppy on the farm and relayed the message to her father to have them name it. She thought about what she would like to eat when she got back to the farm, and looked forward to eating rice with milk and sugar. Ernie determined the best place for her recovery was back in Portales on the farm.

Even though the sickness had a way of breaking her physically and emotionally, and although she was weak, she had not lost her sense of humor.

It is hereby certified that (name) Ernest Bonaventure BONAN, (rate ~~yeo~~), (serial number) 976 49 97, has been on duty outside the continental limits of the United States for not less than twelve consecutive months and on the expiration of his leave will be assigned to duty outside the continental limits of the United States.

~~Lt. (jg) D-V(S) USNR~~
Receiving Officer

Ernie is pictured here in various stages of his military career, possibly while Pat was living in New Mexico.

Before he had established leave of absence in order to be there with Pat, Ernie was on a naval ship out in the middle of the South Pacific, and was deeply concerned for his little girl. He wrote out of his concern, to cheer her with his own poetry.

My Little Darling:

A poem just for you---

While standing guard o'er my Regiment
Proudly alert and alone
Fare attuned to the nite sounds
My thoughts wander lovingly home.
Home where my little loved one
Waits so patient and brave
Awaiting the day when her Daddy
Comes sailing home on the waves.
Never was there a Daddy
Who had more to fight for than I,
The sweet little "Princess Patricia":
For her I would willingly die.
The men in the Regiment sleeping,
In mud holes- in tents and on floors
Smile and stir in the moonlite
And whispers mingle in with their snores.
And as I look around in the shadows,
Searching the jungle space-
Up comes a cloud out of nowhere
And in it is her little face.
And I see the tear and the smile there-
And the longing in the depth of her eyes;
Those little red lips that call 'Daddy'
With a smile that ends with a sigh-
And I pray that God keeps you safe
'Til I get home from these shores--
And with His help and His Grace,
We can carry on as before.
And standing Guard o'er the Regiment
Alert-- but no more alone--
We smile at them together
As they lay dreaming of home

Daddy

Third Grade Class of St. Mary's
School in Muskegon, Michigan,
in 1946.

After the war, Ernie and his "Little Bug," "Patty" returned to Muskegon, Michigan.

Pat attended grade school at St. Mary's School in Muskegon. In the years following, she became a member of the American Legion Auxiliary from Nov. 30, 1946- 1947, and was in the Merritt Lamb Unit # 9 Department of Michigan.

Pat's had many cousins, out of them all she found a familiar friend, Rose Marie Moran- who was Pat's cousin by her dad's brother, Cyril. An office worker for the railroad. (Rose Marie is pictured on the left in the first row of St. Mary's Third Grade Class of 1946- Pat is on the end of the third row, left).

Rose Marie stated in a telephone interview, "We did grow up together. We were friends with the radio a lot, and we were riding bikes all the time. Our family lived right across the street from them. We used to live downtown right across the street from Hackley College, a big beautiful stone school. We'd go swinging at the park there, Hackley Park, until we moved away." Rose Marie got married and moved to Florida.

Charles H. Hackley, one of the millionaires of the lumber era, had turned from the lumber industry, which had depleted the forests in Muskegon area, to developing industry and giving back to the community. He donated Hackley Library and Hackley Park to the city in 1890. It has an 18 ft. high soldier's monument in the center. The entrance to the park has statues of Farragut, Sherman, Grant and Lincoln. The park is a 3.5 acre soldiers' memorial. Ceremonies, rallies, concerts, and a yearly art fair are offered there for cultural entertainment, as well as Parties in the Park. Hackley Park is bounded by Webster and Clay Streets, and 3rd and 4th Streets, downtown, at 350 W. Webster Ave.

Up until 1945 the fishing in lake Michigan was approximately 6.0 million pounds of lake trout per year. It is likely that some of Ernie Moran's brothers were fishermen. Frank Moran was employed by the Pere Marquette Railroad, which debuted during this period, Some of the other Moran brothers may have also worked to improve the infrastructure. Rose Marie's father, Cyril, was a railroad man, as well.

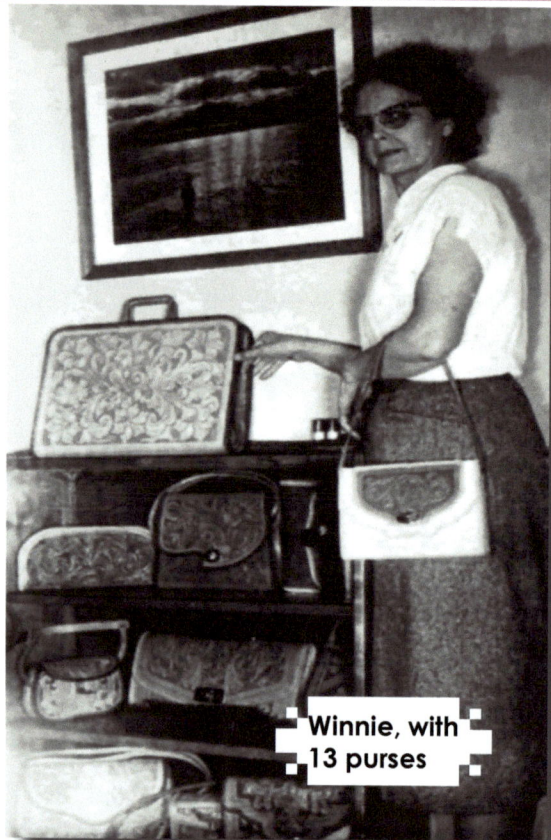

Winnie, with 13 purses

Winifred Moran

Pictured: Ernie Moran and Winifred Gregg at their wedding with the best man and the maid of honor.

Ernie met Winifred Gregg at an ice cream shop, where they were introduced by Agnes, Rose Marie's mother.

Winifred was born on September 5, 1909 near Lake City, Michigan. Her maiden name was Yeager, before her first marriage. Her parents were Harve and Laura Yeager. She had a sister- Edla Ruggles of Illinois, and a brother, George.

Ernie and Winifred got married on June 19, 1948, in Holton, Michigan. They lived at 2677 W. Memorial Drive, in Muskegon.

Winifred's daughter, Maxine, who was married to Fred Whight, became Ernie's second daughter.

Pat welcomed her new mother and sister into the family. Ernie and Winnie lived on 85 Hartford St. in Muskegon.

Winnie was employed by Sealed Power for 42 years and was a member of the UAW. She served the union for many years throughout her life. She also enjoyed being in card clubs, and was a member of the Muskegon Trinity Lutheran Church.

Her travels through life included going to Alaska with Ernie, as well as Hawaii, Hong Kong, and the Aleutian Islands.

Call of Navy Still Strong For 'Old Chief'

A sign maker by trade but a military man at heart is Ernest B. Moran, the veteran chief petty officer who just shipped over for another four-year tour with the U. S. Navy Reserve.

In a way it's a bit flattering to the Navy to have Chief Moran aboard. Veteran of experience in the Army, Air Force, Coast Guard and Seabees as well as the Navy, he appears destined to finish out his career with the bluejackets, apparently by preference.

Moran

* * *

CHIEF MORAN is a veteran of both World Wars and returned to active duty during the Korean conflict. During the first World War he saw duty on the Mexican border, served in Army cavalry units and was a member of the Air Force when it was still part of the Army Signal Corps.

He was a member of the Hawaiian Territorial Guard residing in Honolulu when Pearl Harbor was attacked, after which he joined the Coast Guard as a special investigator on the West Coast. Resigning from the Coast Guard, he enlisted in the Seabees and wound up on the staff of Gen. Douglas MacArthur as chief cartographer.

* * *

AT WAR'S end he returned to Muskegon and joined the new Naval Reserve Unit where he served as chief master at arms, recruit instructor and an unofficial recruiter. He requested active duty immediately after war broke out in Korea but didn't get a billet until January of 1951 when he reported in California. He was then shipped to Adak in charge of housing and furniture warehousing; then sent to the Phillipines where he was in charge of recreation, the enlisted men's club and where he performed special duty in the art section.

Separated from active duty in 1953, he rejoined the Muskegon Reserve unit where he has now signed for another enlistment.

In business life Mr. Moran is manager of the Muskegon Neon Sign Company and makes his home with his wife at 85 Hartford street.

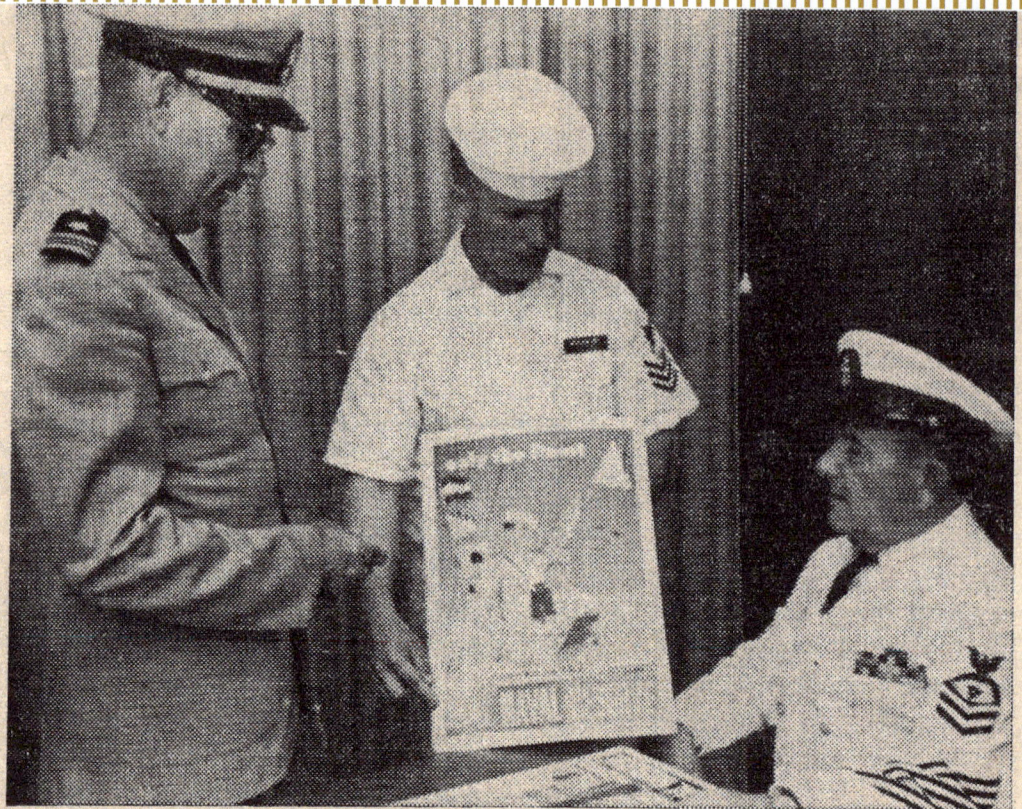

Salty . . . Three top touters for the Navy are in action here today, charting a campaign for recruits to bolster Muskegon's Naval Reserve Division. Looking over recruiting lures are Lt. Cmdr. Harold Minard, in charge of the division; Radioman First Class G. A. Nousain and Chief Ernie Moran, who was

Ernie Moran in his remodeled kitchen.

Ernie Moran

Ernie Moran with his car.

Navy Seeks To Bolster Its Ranks

Muskegon's Naval Reserve Division, its complement down to only two-thirds strength, set sail today on an intensive campaign to strengthen its ranks and revitalize its training program.

Spurred by new community interest in the Navy, rising out of the Seaway Festival visit here of the Blue Angels and the Chuting Stars, Lt. Cmdr. Harold Minard said the division will seek to get back to peak strength of 150 enlisted men and officers. Ranks have slumped to 100.

Recalled to active duty to lead the recruiting campaign is veteran Chief Petty Officer Ernie Moran. Assisted by Radioman First Class G. A. Nousain, Chief Moran will concentrate on enlistment of June high school graduates and other young men. The Naval Reserve enlistment program offers recruits two years of active duty and six years of service in the reserve. Numerous occupational fields are open under the training program.

Training sessions are held Tuesday nights at the Division Training Center on the Lake Michigan channel. Interested young men are invited to visit

Ernie went on active duty during the Korean War in January 1951. He was placed in charge of housing and furniture warehousing in Adak, Alaska. Then he was in recreation, the enlisted men's club in the Philippines where he performed special duty in the art section.

Ernie later served on the new Naval Reserve Unit, as Chief Master at Arms, recruiting instructor, and unofficial recruiter. He was a recruiter at various times throughout his military career

In Recognition of Outstanding Service
to the

United States Navy
Recruiting Service

this

Certificate of Appreciation

is hereby awarded to

Ernest B. Moran

THROUGH your public-spirited cooperation with the Navy Recruiting Service, you have contributed immeasurably in furthering the excellent relations between the United States Navy and the people of your community.

Your individual efforts will stand as a splendid example of initiative, devotion and loyalty to the best interests of the Navy.

In recognition of these services rendered so unselfishly, this Certificate of Appreciation is presented this 9th day of April 19 58 .

H. C. QUAST, CDR, USNR
CinC, NRS&ONOP, Chicago, Ill.

NAVPERS-36092   B39848

April 1952 Murals at Marine Club by E.B. Moran-BMTC for the U.S. Naval Station in Adak, Alaska. RELEASED publishing credit:"OFFICIAL PHOTOGRAPH U. S. NAVY"

In 1952, Ernie went on active duty to Adak, Alaska, Chief Ernie Moran worked for Collateral Furniture and built furniture for the U.S. Navy. Ernie is pictured on the opposite page with furniture that he created for the Division in Adak, in order for them to perform their duties. Prior to that he was Chief Carpenter's Mate in the United States Navy.

March of 1946 Ernest was the Chief Carpenter's Mate in the United States Navy. From then on, Ernest created wood furnishings. Photo Credits: U. S. Navy

Jethro Shaw

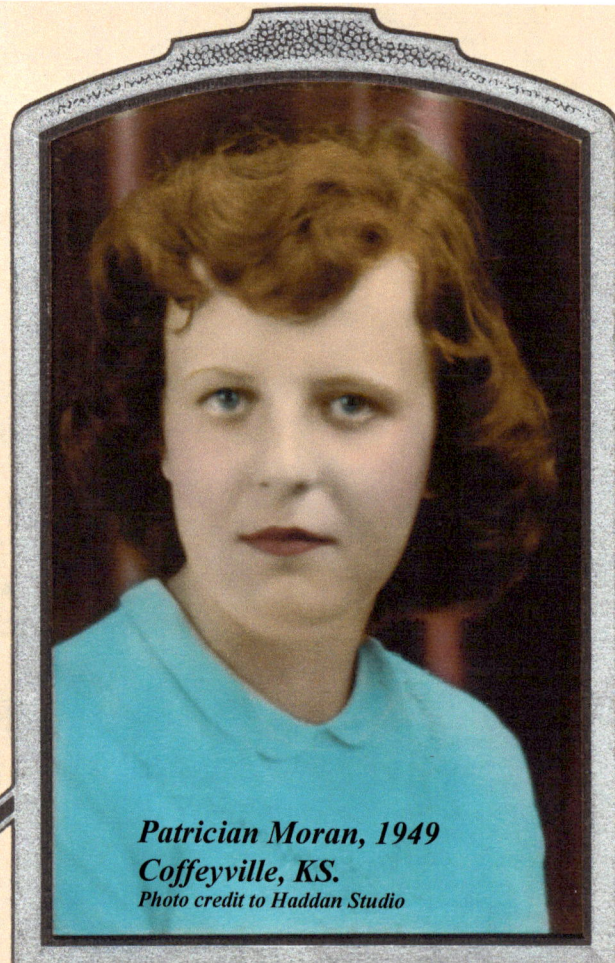

Patrician Moran, 1949
Coffeyville, KS.
Photo credit to Haddan Studio

Pat Moran

1948   Haddan Studio, Coffeyville, Kans.

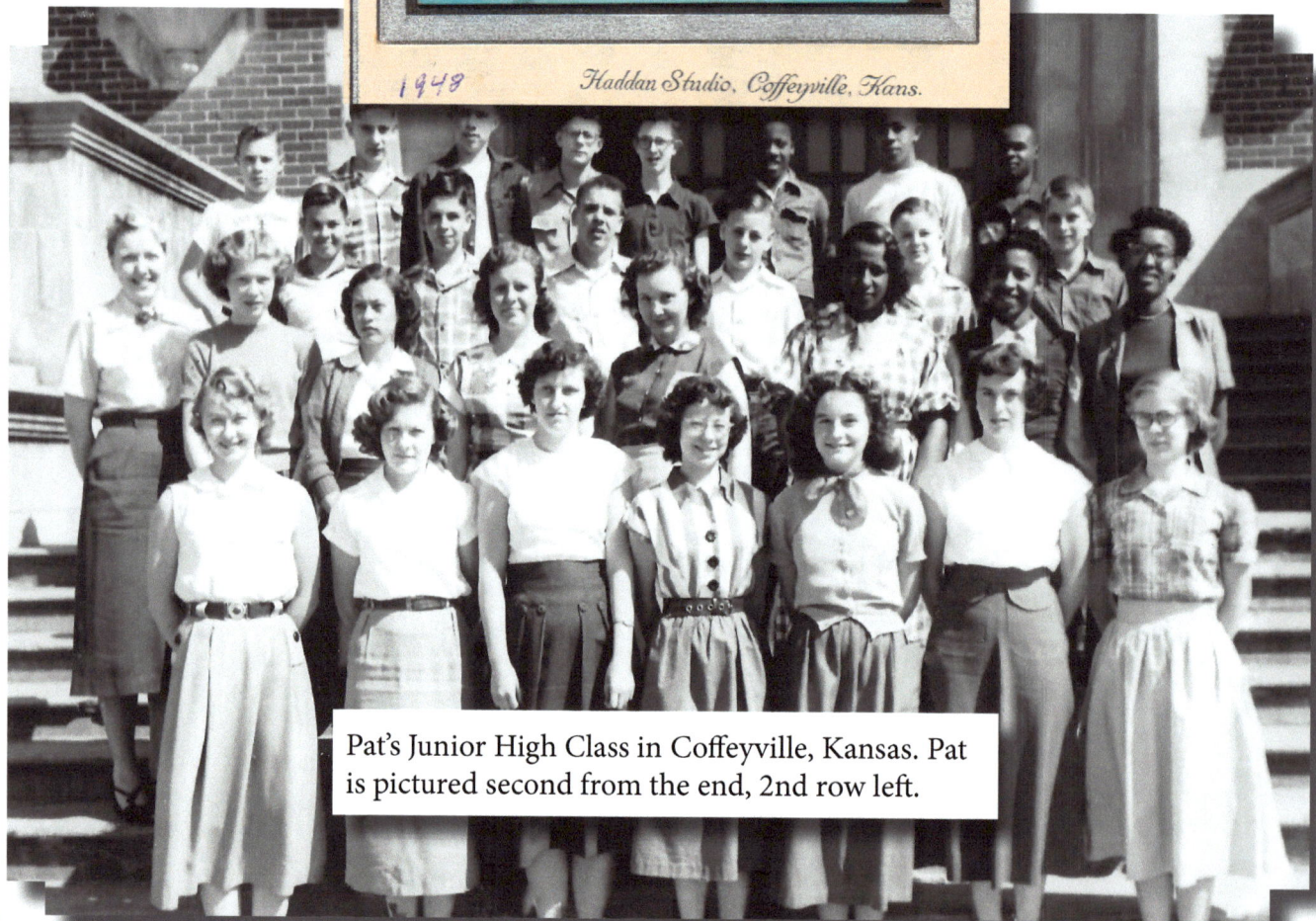

Pat's Junior High Class in Coffeyville, Kansas. Pat is pictured second from the end, 2nd row left.

During the school year, Pat attended St. Mary's Catholic School in Muskegon. In the summer months Pat would vacation with "Aunt" and "Uncle" Davis in Coffeyville, Kansas. They commuted to their farm in Tyro, Kansas.

One summer she stayed at home and felt very lonely with little to entertain her. She didn't enjoy canning corn, but she did enjoy embroidery work to keep busy. She preferred being at the farm where she would swim in the pool, take care of the animals, or go fishing, and if she wished, she'd catch a Greyhound bus to town and go shopping or to the show.

Pat left also, for Coffeyville to stay with the Davis's and attended Jr. High School school there.

When Patricia graduated, she became a long distance telephone operator at General Telephone Company, in Muskegon.

On November 20, 1952, Pat and Jethro Shaw were engaged to be married. Jethro, the son of Pauline Shaw, was from Shenandoah, Iowa. He and Pat had become life long friends, since they first saw each other in New Mexico. At the time they had met, Pat was about 9 or 10. She was hanging upside down, doing gymnastics when they met at Jethro's Uncle Jerome and Aunt Viola's farm.

Miss Moran, J.E. Shaw Wed In Indiana

Patricia Grace Moran, daughter of Mr. and Mrs. Ernest B. Moran, 85 Hartford street, was married June 27 to Jethro E. Shaw, son of Mrs. Pauline Shaw of Shenandoah, Ia.

E. L. Kingsafer of South Bend, Ind., performed the ceremony in South Bend, to which the bride's parents were the only witnesses. For her wedding, the bride wore a navy dress and accessories with a corsage of Remembrance roses. The bridegroom is with the U. S. Air Force on duty in Alexandria, La., as crew chief of a jet squadron.

Following the double-ring ceremony, the couple left for Chicago, returning Thursday for a reception at the home of the bride's parents, at which 50 relatives and close friends were greeted by the newly-married couple.

The bridegroom returned to his base on Friday, but Mrs. Shaw will continue to live in Muskegon, where she is employed by the General Telephone Company.

On June 27, 1953, Pat and Jethro were married in South Bend, Indiana, by E. L. Kingsafer. Pat wore a navy dress and corsage of remembrance roses. After a short honeymoon to Chicago, they attended a wedding reception of about 50 friends and relatives, then Pat went back to work in Muskegon as telephone receptionist, while Jethro went back to active duty in the Air Force. Jethro had spent all he had left on the wedding and honeymoon, so he borrowed money from his uncle, Ira Johnson, to get to Alexandria, Virginia, where he would become a Jet Squadron Crew Chief.

LICENSE VOID 60 DAYS FROM DATE OF ISSUANCE UNDER CHAPTER 100, PAGE 154, AMENDED ACTS 1939

Marriage License

No. 1155

The State of Indiana
To Any Person Empowered by Law to Solemnize Such Marriage, Greetings:

You are hereby authorized to join together as Husband and Wife

Jethro E. Shaw

and

Patricia G. Moran

and of this, together with your Certificate of Marriage, make due return within THREE DAYS, according to the laws of the State of Indiana.

WITNESS, Marcella Brown, Clerk of the St. Joseph Circuit Court and the Seal thereof hereto affixed at South Bend, Indiana,

this 27 day of June A. D., 1953

By _____ Marcella Brown _____ Clerk

_____ Helen Elder _____ Deputy

The above License and the following Certificate must be returned to the Clerk's office within THREE DAYS with the blanks filled with the NAMES and DATES, and signed by the person solemnizing Marriage. —Acts 1913, Page 680.

Marriage Certificate

State of Indiana, St. Joseph County, ss.

I, E. L. Kingsafer of said County, do hereby certify that on the 27th day of June A. D., 1953, I joined in marriage Jethro E. Shaw and Patricia G. Moran by authority of License from the Clerk of St. Joseph Circuit Court.

Given under my hand this Eighth day of June, 19 53

South _____ E. L. Kingsafer

Place of Marriage _____ Minister of the Gospel or Justice of the Peace

Pat bought a trailer for $300.00, and Jethro relocated them to the England Air Force Base, where Jethro was stationed and began his assignment in the 390th Division of the Air Force in Alexander, Louisiana,beginning July 1, 1953. On the side, Jethro took on cleaning the bath and laundry house as well as mowing yards, in order to purchase a new car.

Pat had her first child- a boy, when she was years 19 years old, Ernest Eugene Shaw, born in August in Pineville, Louisiana, a year after they were married. Some time shortly afterward, Jethro reenlisted and was planning to head for Aviano, Italy. In December of 1955, Jethro's mom and Paul, his brother helped move Jethro, Pat and baby Eugene to their new home with the larger trailer that Jethro had purchased, to 213 N. Broad Street in Shenandoah, Iowa- across the street from where Pauline lived.
Jethro was sent to Germany and soon returned to Iowa where he was assigned to the base in Sioux City.

Almost exactly two years after their first child, a second son- Kenneth Howard Shaw was born at Offutt Air Force Base, Nebraska.

Jethro upgraded the trailer to a larger two bedroom model, moved to Dewey Trailer Park, in Sergeant Bluff, Iowa in August 1956.

Then Gary Wayne Shaw, their third son was born in the spring of '59, at the Sioux City, Iowa hospital.

Jethro was transferred to Richards- Gebaur A.F.B. in Belton, Missouri, and a larger trailer was in order for a larger family of boys, so in March of 1959, they moved to Olsen Trailer Park, Belton, Missouri. Paula Elizabeth was born in January two years later and David Alan was born two more years later, in May. of 1963.

August 1963 brought them back to rural Bingham, Iowa, near Shenandoah, where Jethro and his mother had owned some property.

Pat had an interesting ride when a tornado picked up the trailer and moved it eight feet, while she was cooking, and spilled the food.

In September 1964 the family traveled to a new location at 36 Sagebrush Lane, in Del Rio, Texas.

From November 1968 until June 1969 they lived once again in Southwest Iowa, at Box 232, Farragut.

Then, until October 1971, they lived in a home at 2309 Mohave Avenue, Glendale, Arizona,- near Phoenix while Jethro was stationed at Luke Air Force Base.

Ernie enrolled in the Fraternal Order of the Eagles about the same time that Pat and Jethro got engaged in 1952.

He separated from active duty in 1953, then re-enlisted in the Naval Reserve Unit in Muskegon. Ernie spent his time in the Naval Reserve as a mobile recruiter. He recruited and trained new recruiting officers, and became the Organized Surface Division 9-103 most enthusiastic member. He recruited his nephew, Bill (the son of Cyril Moran) for the Navy, for the second time after he served - the first was in 1048, while Bill was still in high school.

His dedication showed in that he decorated the Naval Reserve Training Center and the local Coast Guard station. He worked in the design and drafting section at the Great Lakes.

On the side, Ernie made and repaired toys for the NRTC carpenter shop for Muskegon underprivileged children. He dedicated time to this during the Christmas season and blessed many children.

Ernie also began his design and sign shop, again-The Muskegon Neon Sign Company.

Here, on the opposite page, are pictures of Ernest and some of his graphic design work.

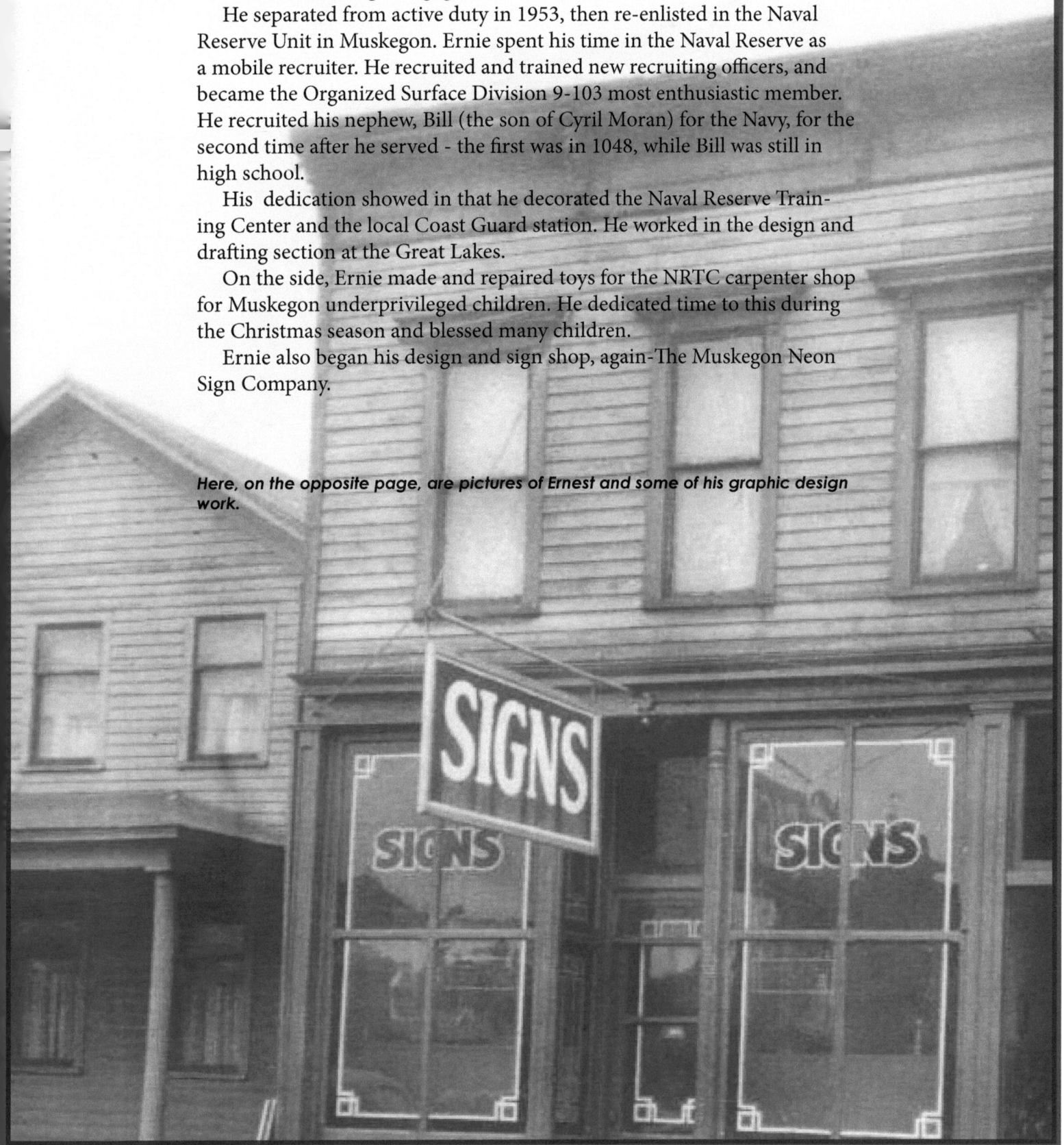

The pictures on these two pages are of Ernest and Winnie during their lifetime together.

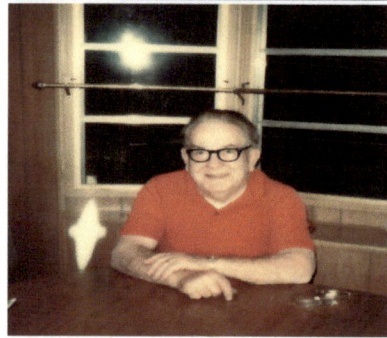

Holiday
Greetings and
"Aloha"
From Utility Squadron One

MORAN, MR.
ERNEST B.
35 Hartford

Mr. Ernest Moran, age 75, born June 1, 1903 in Ludington, Mich. He had lived most of his adult life in the Muskegon area. He married the former Winifred Gregg in Muskegon, June 19, 1948. He was a self-employed sign writer. Mr. Moran retired from the U.S. Navy after 37½ years of service. He was a member of the Veterans of W.W. I Post No. 328, DAV Scott Wood Post No. 11 and the V.F.W. No. 446. The survivors are his wife Winifred, 2 daughters, Mrs. Jethro (Patricia) Shaw of Iowa and Mrs. Fred (Maxine) Whight of Albany, NY, 2 sisters, Mrs. Ruth Byers of California and Mrs. Grace Cone of Buchanan, Mi., 10 grandchildren and 2 great-grandchildren. The funeral service will be held at 2 P.M. Sunday in the Young Funeral Home, Rev. Norbert Leyrita officiating. Friends may call at the Young Funeral Home beginning this evening at 7 P.M. The family will be present Saturday 2-4 and 7-9 P.M. Memorial tributes may be made to the charity of your choice.

— Young

Ernie was honorably discharged from the Armed Forces of United States Navy on February 5, 1955 of the USN & MCRTC in Muskegon, Michigan. He served various dates, from April 30, 1948. He served as Chief Draftsman in the USNR until December 6th, 1962.

He served as Chief Master at Arms, recruiting instructor in Muskegon, and was attributed to be the unofficial recruiter of the unit. Ernie retired on April 1, 1966.

Ernie was born June 1, 1903, in Ludington, Michigan, At the age of 75, his heart failed him. He passed away on Feb. 23, 1979, having arteriosclerotic heart disease. He had two sisters remaining out of the original 17 siblings, six of whom died at birth. They were Ruth Byers of California, and Grace Cone of Buchanan, Michigan.

At the time of his passing, Ernie had ten grandchildren and two great-grandchildren. His wife Winifred Gregg, also survived him. His remains are located in the Holton Cemetery in Holton Township, Michigan.

His memory was honored by the United States of America for his devoted and selfless consecration to the service of the country in the Armed Forces of the United States, signed by President Jimmy Carter.

He was a member of the Veterans of WW1 post No. 328, the DAV Scott Wood Post No. 11, and the V. F. W. No. 446.

Winifred Gregg passed away July 23, 2006, with 5 grandchildren, 8 great grandchildren, and one great- great granddaughter at the time. Her grave is in Holton Cemetery, in Holton, Michigan.

These are the many faces Of Ernest Moran

Posing with clocks Or furniture he created, At home or In full decoration of his years in service to our country, Ernest is ready to march in the parade.

Ernest B. Moran with the sword that he was gifted to honor his service.

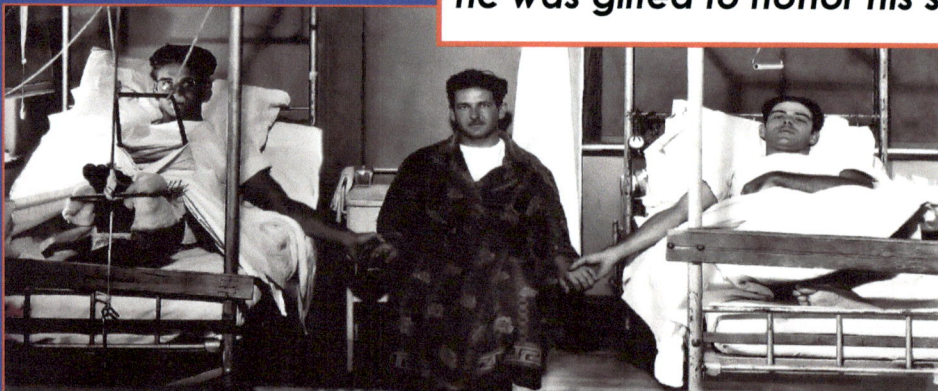

Ernie is pictured in the hospital showing moral support to his comrades at war, during two different times of his life.

(UNTITLED POEM)
        By a friend of Ernie Moran
That man is a success, Who has lived well,
Laughed often and loved sound.
Who has gained the respect of intelligent men
And the love of children
Who has filled his niche, and accomplished his task
Who leaves the world better than he found it-
Whether by an improved poppy, a perfect poem,
Or a rescued soul.
Who never lacked appreciation of earth's beauty
Or failed to express it, who looked for the best in
Others and gave the best he had.
Ernie, as we knew and loved him, was a man of all
These virtues and more. To know him was to love him.
He was a confidant, our advisor, sometimes our
Father confessor. No task was too difficult for him,
And on many occasions we came to him with our
Broken
Mementos to be repaired. He would amuse us with his
Stories,
And sometimes we surely felt he must have kissed the
Blarney
Stone, only to find out later that his stories were true.
He was a gifted and artistic man who shared his talents
With
Others.
Ernie was a devoted husband, father, and grandfather.
While some of us are too busy to express affection,
Ernie
Never left the house without kissing his wife goodbye.
Much of his life was devoted to the service of his
Country.
He wore his uniform proudly, the hash marks denoting
Decades
Of service, and the gleaming rows of campaign rib-
bons earned
In his two World Wars and the Korean Conflict. He
Was presented
An ornate sword by his fellow Navy men when retire-
ment
Finally came.
We, who remain to carry on, should not think of our
Shipmates as departed from us, but rather as having
Been
Transferred to a celestial ship or station, where we
Hope
All of us may be Shipmates again.

Marshal of the Day

He wears his uniform proudly . . . the hash marks made . . . decades of service . . . the campaign ribbons earned in . . . the . . . World War and the Korean Conflict . . . presented by fellow Navymen . . . He was at Pearl Harbor when the attack came . . . has seen service around the globe. Few are better qualified to lead Muskegon's Memorial Day Parade than Chief Ernest B. Moran, who will head the line march Saturday. We agree wholeheartedly.

Grand Marshal Of the Parade, Ernest Bonaventure Moran, bearing the sword he received from the Navy when he retired. This news clipping bears the signatures of his comrades and friends.

A graphic that Ernie designed.

Thanks be unto God
Which always causes us to
Triumph in Christ

Purple Columbine

resolved to win

MOTHER
BETTY MORAN
1907 — 1935

ERNEST B.
MORAN
1903 — 1979

Together, Jethro and Pat had five children: Erney, Kenny, Gary, Paula and David, and Pat was devoted to making her family and home the priority of her life.

Jethro served our country, in the military for 20 years. Then in 1971, their family moved to Farragut, Iowa. He worked at Eaton's Transmission Corporation in Shenandoah, Iowa starting on Nov. 23, 1971 until he retired on March 6, 1992. Jethro was a faithful and skilled worker at Eaton Corporation, and was commended for not missing a day of work during his many years of service there.

Jethro and Pat traveled to Newfoundland, Prince Edward Island, and southern California. Branson, Missouri, with its music and live entertainment was their favorite vacationing spot. Together Pat and Jethro enjoyed life.

ANNIVERSARY... Jethro and Pat Shaw will celebrated their 60th anniversary on June 27, 2013. In honor of this occasion their family is hosting a card shower. Cards may be sent to Jethro and Pat at 2019 US Hwy 59, Shenandoah, Iowa 51601.

Patricia Grace Shaw passed away on October 22, 2017, at the glorious age of 82. She was grandmother of 17, and with 15 great grandchildren.

Of the years of her life, Patricia has left a legacy to her family that cannot be compared to earthly riches. Many times, she encountered hardship that others would not have survived. Perhaps, her life was spared for a reason. It was not to share talents of artistic nature like her father, or eloquent words. It seems that she had other things to share with her survivors, like love and courage, faith in Christ, and grace to do life, well.

Pat was laid to rest on Saturday, October 28, 2017. Her remains are located in Rose Hill Cemetery, in Shenandoah, Iowa.

CHRIST HAS DONE FOR ME

Written by Pat Shaw

Jesus Christ as my Savior
Salvation,
Forgiveness for my sins
Life Eternal.
A wonderful husband, love
Children
My health
Friends
A home, food, money
Average intelligence

Acknowledgements

Http://lighthousefriends.com/light.asp?ID=191

UNITED STATES ARMY IN WORLD WAR I I The War in the Pacific THE FALL OF THE PHILIPPINES; Louis Morton; CENTER OF MILITARY HISTORY UNITED STATES, printed 1953

Http://www.muskegon-mi.gov/community/history/

Http://www.mlive.com/news/muskegon/index.ssf/2014/09/not_your_parents_downtown_time.html

Https://www.matson.com/bos/history

Https://www.newspapers.com/newspage/1105848/

www.mlive.com/news/muskegon/index.ssf/2012/12/look_back_pearl_harbor.html
Http://iagenweb.org/page/obituaries/2014/Page-029.html

The content in these pages are from the many news clippings, collections of photographs, awards, certificates, or personal letters and writings of Patricia Shaw, from collections and testimony of Jethro Shaw, as well as the word of Rose Marie Pitts. General information was found in the World Book Encyclopedia.

Permission to print military photos and documents was obtained from the U.S. Department of Defense Book PR Division. Credit is given to the United States Navy, the United States Army, and the United States Coast Guard.

Some newspaper articles, sources are unknown.
Credit is given to:
The Ludington Times: Horse and Rider Off On Long Trip Around the Country
The Muskegon Chronicle : articles on page 53.
The Honolulu Star: Leeward Oahu Sunrise Service
The Star Bulletin
Shenandoah Valley News Today: Pat and Jethro Shaw 2013, 60th Wedding Anniversary

During research, interesting facts were found in Chronicling America's on-line database from the National Archives in the Library of Congress. They may or may not relate to Ernest B. Moran in our memoir.

In the annual election of officers of Typographical Union No. 136 held Sunday June 7, William Moran was sergeant at arms Duluth, MN.
The labor world. (Duluth, Minn.), 20 June 1896. Chronicling America: Historic American Newspapers. Lib. of Congress. <http://chroniclingamerica.loc.gov/lccn/sn78000395/1896-06-20/ed-1/seq-4/>

L'Anse, L.S. Michigan Nov 7, 1914 Ernest Moran is listed as being on the Township School of Barage County, Mi. Roll of Honor for 7th grade. As well as Helen Moran of the 4rd grade and Annabelle Moran 1st grade.

Willmington: Ernest Moran has finished work for the Hoosac Lumber Co. at Heartwellville, and has accepted a position at the Ludington Wooden Ware Co. 05-09-1918

The Brattleboro daily reformer. (Brattleboro, Vt.), 09 May 1918. Chronicling America: Historic American Newspapers. Lib. of Congress. <http://chroniclingamerica.loc.gov/lccn/sn86071593/1918-05-09/ed-1/seq-8/>

An Ernest Moran was recruited and enlisted into the calvary in Washington D.C June 30, 1917

The Washington herald. (Washington, D.C.), 30 June 1917. Chronicling America: Historic American Newspapers. Lib. of Congress. <http://chroniclingamerica.loc.gov/lccn/sn83045433/1917-06-30/ed-1/seq-3/>

Dec 24, 1920; Dec 30, 1921
enrollment of Ernest Moran in little Falls, MN. School.